W9-CYA-789

HANS AND SOPHIE SCHOLL

HANS AND SOPHIE SCHOLL

LARA SAHGAL
AND TOBY AXELROD

Published in 2016 by The Rosen Publishing Group, Inc.
29 East 21st Street, New York, NY 10010

Library of Congress Cataloging-in-Publication Data

Sahgal, Lara, author.
 Hans and Sophie Scholl / Lara Sahgal and Toby Axelrod.—First edition.
    pages cm. — (The Holocaust (Series title))
 Includes bibliographical references and index.
 ISBN 978-1-4994-6244-9 (library bound)
 1. Weisse Rose (Resistance group—History—Juvenile literature.
 2. Universität München—Riot, 1943—Juvenile literature. 3. Anti-Nazi
 movement—Germany—Juvenile literature. 4. World War, 1939-1945—
 Underground movements—Germany—Munich—Juvenile literature.
 I. Axelrod, Toby, author. II. Title.
 DD256.3.S165 2015
 940.53'1832--dc23

                                                          2015032166

Manufactured in China

CONTENTS

INTRODUCTION

They went to school. They went to concerts. They hung out with friends. In these respects, it might seem that youth who grew up in Nazi Germany had ordinary child-hoods. But with the rise of the National Socialist, or Nazi, Party and its leader, Adolf Hitler, little in Germany remained ordinary. The Nazi agenda was deeply entrenched in all aspects of German society, and even young people were not immune. In fact, Hitler's vision for Germany depended on his ability to indoctrinate youth to Nazi ideology.

Propaganda was one of the most powerful tools at the disposal of the Nazis—false or exaggerated information that touted Nazi ideals and disparaged others permeated German culture. Propaganda could take just about any form of communication, from books

The main square of Ludwig Maximilian University in Munich is called Geschwister-Scholl-Platz, named in honor of Hans and Sophie Scholl. It is where this memorial to the White Rose is located.

to newspapers to radio. It even infiltrated class-rooms. Teachers were required to incorporate Nazi values in their lessons and encourage anti-Semitism among students. History lessons glorified German conquests and leaders and diminished other countries, races, and ideologies. Biology classes taught students that the "Aryan" race was superior to all others. Other science classes emphasized principles of military and warfare.

Outside of the classroom, many students joined Hitler youth groups—organizations that set out to turn young people into loyal and unquestioning members of the Nazi Party. Eventually, young people between the ages of 10 and 17 were required to join one of these groups. There was little room for criticism, disagreement, or dissent.

Yet, despite the drastic consequences, many Germans did dissent from Nazi policies. The members of the White Rose movement were among those in this category. Many of the members of the White Rose, including siblings Hans and Sophie Scholl, came of age in the political and social climate created by the Third Reich. They dutifully attended youth groups but started sensing early on the oppressiveness of the Nazi regime.

As students at the Ludwig Maximilian University of Munich, the Scholl siblings met and befriended some like-minded thinkers who opposed Nazi policies and were horrified by Nazi atrocities, including the mass exterminations being carried out against Jews and other groups.

Together, these students formed the White Rose resistance movement in 1942.

Meeting in secret, often not even telling their families, they decided to take action. Between 1942 and 1943, the group's members clandestinely printed and distributed around Munich and other cities antiwar and anti-Nazi leaflets. Cutting through the noise of propaganda messages, these powerful documents strove to awaken the conscience of Germans about crimes being committed in their name. Although they appealed to fellow Germans to engage in passive, non-violent resistance, the members knew their actions would be considered treason and could result in death sentences if they were found out.

Tragically, the White Rose members were ultimately caught. Some were imprisoned. Others, including both Hans and Sophie Scholl, were executed and did not live to see their vision—the end of the war and the downfall of the Nazi Party—realized. Hans and Sophie are often credited with spearheading the movement, but every member of the White Rose was crucial to the effort, and each one remains an enduring symbol of the power of resistance in the face of injustice and oppression. Although young—many hadn't even hit their thirtieth birthdays when caught—these courageous individuals are testament that ordinary people can make extraordinary differences.

CHAPTER ONE

BUILDUP TO WORLD WAR II

In the wake of its defeat in World War I, Germany struggled politically and economically. Amongst its citizens, morale was low. Many resented the victory of Allied powers—including the United States—and felt that Germany should not have to owe the victors millions of dollars in reparations. In the early 1930s, the whole world was struck by economic depression. More than 30 percent of Germany's workforce was unemployed. The combination of events and circumstances created a climate that was ripe for a radical solution—and a radical leader.

In 1933, Adolf Hitler became chancellor of Germany and ushered in the age of the Third Reich, as his regime was known. Hitler's political party, the National Socialists, or Nazis, had won more votes than any other party in the election of November 1932.

Adolf Hitler's rise to power was facilitated by his ability to build nationalistic pride at a time when Germany faced issues such as high unemployment and economic depression.

THE RISE OF THE THIRD REICH

Hitler promised to create jobs and make Germany strong again. He claimed that Germans—Aryans, he called them—were superior to other peoples and were destined to be part of a great and powerful nation. He blamed Germany's problems on a tiny portion of its population, the Jews. In his memoir, *Mein Kampf* (*My Struggle*), Hitler wrote that the sole purpose of the state was to guard the purity of the German race.

Once in power, Hitler began to change Germany's government. It had been democratic; now, Hitler gathered all the power of the government unto himself. He dissolved the Reichstag (parliament) and, after the death of the nation's president, the war hero Paul von Hindenburg, in August 1934, joined the powers of the office of the president and the chancellor together. As supreme head of the government, Hitler's title was Führer, or leader. Eventually, he would build up Germany's military forces and use them to achieve his goal of building a larger Germany, which in his vision included most of eastern Europe.

Hitler paid special attention to indoctrinating German youth. He encouraged teenagers to visit the jail in Landsberg where he had been kept after his arrest in 1923 for trying to overthrow the government and where he had written *Mein Kampf*. Scouting clubs, called the Hitler Youth, made special pilgrimages to Landsberg for this purpose.

Later, these teens would become soldiers in Hitler's military machine. While uplifting German youth who fit the Aryan stereotype, Hitler enacted laws that curtailed the rights of Jewish citizens.

On September 1, 1939, Germany invaded Poland. It was the first step of a larger military plan to seize control of much of eastern Europe in

Propaganda posters such as this one were designed to attract young Germans to a Hitler Youth group. Most featured images of Hitler or a swastika, the symbol of the Nazi Party.

order to establish *Lebensraum,* or living space, for Germans. Thus began the Second World War. Slated for extermination were those Hitler considered "inferior:" Jews, Slavs, political dissidents (people opposed to the Nazis, such as Communists), Gypsies or Roma, people who were physically disabled or considered mentally ill, and people who were, or were thought to be, homosexual.

Once the Nazis occupied a country, they started to round up all these so-called undesirables. They were then either killed outright or sent to concentration camps, where they would serve as slave labor until they were killed. By the end of the war, Germany had occupied most of Europe. Ultimately, lands under Nazi domination included Austria, Belgium, Czechoslovakia, Denmark, part of Finland, France, part of Greece, Luxembourg, the Netherlands, Norway, Poland, Serbia, Belarus, Estonia, Latvia, Lithuania, the Ukraine, the western portion of Russia, Romania, Bulgaria, and Italy. Rumors about the mass murder of Jews spread through Europe. Of some nine million Jews who lived in these areas before the war, some six million were killed by the Nazis in mass executions or in the death camps. This genocide is now known as the Holocaust.

Most Germans did not actively resist the dictatorship under which they lived. The great majority enjoyed the benefits of Hitler's policies. He promised more jobs at a time of great unemployment.

Prisoners at the Sachsenhausen concentration camp, like those at other labor camps, were forced to perform back-breaking tasks under extremely harsh conditions.

He told Germans that they were the best people in the world at a time when they felt humiliated and defeated. He nourished the patriotic and nationalistic feelings of many of his countrymen.

GERMAN RESISTANCE

But there were Germans who saw through the Nazi rhetoric of hate. They believed that Hitler was destroying everything good about Germany. They believed it was possible to build a democracy in their country in which people of all ethnic and religious backgrounds could live together.

In the beginning of World War II, the German army was successful, rolling through much of Europe with little real opposition. But gradually, Germany began to lose major battles, and tens of thousands of young soldiers died. At the terrible Battle of Stalingrad (now called Volgograd) in Russia, which lasted from July 1942 until early February 1943, Germany suffered its first major defeat in the war. An estimated 800,000 men in the German forces lost their lives; the Russians lost 1.1 million men.

At that point, even some Germans who *had* liked Hitler became critical. For those who never liked him, it seemed like the right time to try to convince others to oppose the regime. As the war dragged on, consuming lives and taxing the economy, Hitler and his leadership became increasingly worried about dissent. The regime started to crack down harder on critics. It became more and more dangerous to express opposition. People who made jokes about Hitler and were overheard by the wrong person could end up in jail, or even executed. Meanwhile, heavy Allied bombing of German cities had begun early in 1942.

Many Germans, from all walks of life and through various means, resisted Nazi rule. But there were many more who did nothing against the regime. Germans who raised their hands in the Nazi salute by far outnumbered those who raised a fist. Those who struggled did so mostly in vain. Their stories should be seen within the context of their time: at first, general enthusiasm and compliance in the population and later, in the face of atrocities and the flagging war, apathy or paralyzing fear.

In 1933, when Adolf Hitler came to power, Germany's population was approximately 50 million. By the end of World War II, some 40,000 Germans had been executed for taking forbidden political or moral stands. The war, which lasted six years, cost the lives of approximately 50 million people, including the millions of civilians who were killed by the Nazis in mass shootings or in concentration camps.

Within Germany, resistance came from many quarters: the political left and right; the

Claus Schenk Graf von Stauffenberg was a disillusioned officer in the German army who went on to be a principal player in the failed July 20 plot to assassinate Hitler.

labor movement; Christians, Jews, and Quakers; and the military, most notably the final attempt to assassinate Hitler, carried out by Claus Schenk Graf von Stauffenberg on July 20, 1944. In reprisal, more than 4,000 people were executed in the following days, weeks, and months.

In all, more than 5,000 death sentences came from the so-called People's Court, set up in 1934 to counter political resistance. And the special courts condemned thousands more, with no chance for appeal. In addition, hundreds of thousands of Germans spent years locked up as political prisoners. But they ultimately went home.

"The fact that there was any significant opposition is extraordinary," comments Holocaust scholar Jud Newborn, coauthor of *Shattering the German Night*, a book about the White Rose student resistance. "But if more people had been capable of organizing and resisting early on, it's quite likely the regime would never have gone as far as it did. The Nazi government was very attentive to public opinion."

Stars stand out against the blackest night. Such a benign metaphor may seem strange for German resistance against Nazism. But it may be helpful to picture a handful of stars, scattered against a backdrop of profound darkness. Such were the members of the White Rose resistance—a small group of students and teachers in Munich, the city that was the center of the Nazi movement, who wrote and distributed anti-Nazi leaflets throughout Germany and

THE EDELWEISS PIRATES

The members of the White Rose were not the only young people to resist Nazi authority. The term Edelweiss Pirates encompasses various youth groups that sprang up around Germany. It was one of the largest youth resistance movements in Germany. The individuals who belonged to these groups were teens—typically males between the ages of 16 and 18, though some were younger—who refused to participate in Nazi youth groups. They began as groups of working class youth who shared interests, such as music, that were banned under Nazi rule. They usually had an unconventional style of dress— checkered shirts, short trousers, and scarves—and distinguished themselves with a pin of an edelweiss flower on their lapels. They often worked factory or mill jobs during the day, and on their own time enjoyed their personal freedom by exploring the countryside or hanging out in parks and cafés. There was no central organization or even much contact between groups in different cities, but all groups shared a distrust of the Nazi Party. They would engage in vandalism and often clashed with Hitler Youth, usually violently, but as the war intensified, they took more extreme measures.

Some groups would harbor or help individuals who escaped from concentration camps. Others destroyed railroads, factories, and German war muni-tions. Some stole arms or made armed raids in order to sabotage German operations. Those who were caught were imprisoned, sent to a camp, or executed. Only in 2005 were the members officially recognized as "resistance fighters and heroes."

painted anti-Nazi graffiti on buildings in Munich during 1942 and 1943.

THE ROLE OF THE WHITE ROSE

The White Rose became active starting in the summer of 1942, just before the Battle of Stalingrad began. They secretly printed leaflets against Hitler, the government, and the war. Instead of accepting the rules, they fought against them. Instead of accepting Nazi propaganda about the war, they tried to tell the public that the war would be lost.

Hans and Sophie Scholl were siblings who became central members of the White Rose resistance movement, which distributed anti-Nazi leaflets around Munich and other German cities.

Most important, the group wrote in their leaflets about the atrocities being committed against innocent people in the name of Germany. They took a moral stand against Hitler and upheld the hope that humanity would triumph and lead to a better world. It was a world most of them would not live to see.

The main White Rose founders were Munich medical students Hans Scholl, Christoph Probst, Alexander Schmorell, and Helmut Hartert. They were joined by several others, including Hans's younger sister, Sophie. They were inspired by Munich professor of philosophy and musicology Kurt Huber, who was invited to join in the resistance work in December 1942. The movement eventually made contacts in other cities in Germany.

CHAPTER TWO

THE SCHOLL SIBLINGS

Although much about Hans and Sophie Scholl's upbringing seems typical of the Third Reich era, in many ways, they differed from others their age. Their family's influence in shaping their values became clear as they entered adulthood themselves. Each sibling pursued separate interests socially and academically, but converged in their political views. Both Hans and Sophie went on to serve unique roles as White Rose members and were crucial to the movement's successes.

FAMILY LIFE

Robert and Magdalene Scholl met during World War I, when he was serving in a military hospital in Ludwigsburg. Magdalene, whose last name was then Mueller, was a nurse in the same hospital. The two fell in love and were soon married.

They started their family in the small town of Ingersheim on Cralsheim, where Robert was the liberal democratic mayor. Inge, the oldest child, was born in 1917. Hans was born in 1918;

Hans and Sophie Scholl were primarily raised in Ulm, a city in the southwestern part of Germany in the state of Baden-Württemberg.

Elisabeth followed in 1920; Sophie in 1921; and Werner in 1922. Werner would die as a soldier on the Russian front in 1943.

In 1919, the family moved to Forchtenberg, where Robert was also elected mayor. In 1930, after he failed to win re-election, the family moved to Ludwigsburg. Two years later, they moved to Ulm, a city of some 60,000 on the Danube River in southwestern Germany. There, Robert Scholl started a business as a financial and tax adviser. The family lived in a large, rented apartment on Cathedral Square.

Sophie was a good student with special talent in art and music. She loved fairy tales, and the illustrations she made for a friend's copy of *Peter Pan* were published after her death. Swimming was a favorite childhood pastime, and she later became a fine dancer. She kept a diary and wrote letters and stories. Later, discussing literature with friends was something both she and Hans would enjoy. Friends and family remembered that even as a child, Sophie Scholl was someone who stood up for what she thought was right, even if it meant talking back to an adult.

Shortly after the family moved to Ulm, Germany's postwar experiment with democracy, the Weimar Republic, came to an end. The world economic depression of 1929 had undermined the stability of the government to the extent that by 1932, Adolf Hitler and the Nazis had become the most powerful political entity in Germany.

After Hitler came to power in January 1933, even the lives of children were profoundly affected by the Nazi Party's extremely nationalistic ideals. Like most others their age, the Scholls joined the official Nazi youth organizations—the Hitler Youth and League of German Girls. Sophie was twelve when she joined; Hans was fifteen. At first, the Scholls were enthusiastic members of the Nazi clubs and became leaders. That would change.

The Hitler Youth and League of German Girls were designed to train young people to think along Nazi lines—that Germans and their culture were superior. In some ways, they were more like other youth organizations, offering a chance for boys and girls to go camping or hiking. Later, the National Socialist youth groups tried to control more aspects of the lives of their members—what they wore, their hairstyles, what music they listened to, whom they associated with. Members of the Hitler Youth were also instilled with the desire to fight for the honor of Germany.

The League of German Girls would indoctrinate young girls to Nazi ideology through stories, sports, song, camping, and other activities that were meant to be enjoyable. Later, the girls would learn various home economics skills.

At first, membership in such groups was voluntary, at least legally speaking. But after March 25, 1939, membership was required by law for all "Aryan" youths. By then most other youth organi-

FAMILY INFLUENCE

Acquaintances of the Scholl family have reflected on the critical influence the family environment had on Hans's and Sophie's political and world views. Although both siblings were adults when the White Rose formed, their childhood upbringing and the progressive home environment in which they came of age clearly resonated into their adulthood.

Franz Mueller was a young school friend of the Scholls' who later became involved with the White Rose. He says that Robert and Magdalene had a critical influence on their children and, ultimately, on the White Rose group. "The Scholl family was very important," Mueller says. "I don't know of another family in the White Rose that had such a decisive impact on their children's political direction."

"The Scholls' spirit was very open," Mueller remembers. As an example, he explains that the Scholls admired work by artists who were condemned by the Nazis. "In Germany," says Mueller, "if you admired such artists you were considered an outsider, even mentally ill. And this was the Scholl family."

They had a nice apartment, with seven rooms. The children were on the top floor. They had a wonderful library with some books in French. Hans spoke excellent French and when he was a soldier in France he was used as an interpreter.

George Wittenstein had vivid memories of Sophie Scholl, whom he characterized as being "on one hand very serious and yet very fun-loving. It was more than humor. She enjoyed life to the fullest, and simple nature—a bunch of grass or blossoms on the tree, or flowers in the field—could completely change her."

Sophie Scholl was "not very tall, she was handsome, and she was a free-going and moving person," recalls Mueller, who knew Hans better. For him, too, the memories of the Scholls are vivid: "It is not a long time ago . . . for me it is present," he says. "Hans was a very complicated person, very special, different from other guys. He was very highly educated . . . and he had leadership abilities. But Hans did not tell people what to do. He was not so orthodox, saying, 'You have to do this or that.' He saw different possibilities. On top of everything, Hans had no fear. He had no sense of danger. That was very bad. It sounds terrible, but it is a fact. If you have no fear, you can have a clear vision. But it is dangerous."

zations, including one called the German Youth of Nov. 1, 1929, had been outlawed.

Although the German Youth—called d.j.1.11 for short (*Deutsch Jugend* means "German Youth")—professed ideals of nationalism and spiritual and physical development, the group also encouraged members to learn about other cultures through music and literature. The German Youth, which had branches around the country, was banned in 1933. But its influence was profound, in particular on Hans Scholl.

Robert and Magdalene Scholl opposed the National Socialist youth groups but did not prevent their children from joining. Robert Scholl frequently expressed his own liberal views and hoped his children would learn from discussions with him. He was a pacifist who had refused to carry a gun during World War I. He advised his children not to believe everything they heard, and he frequently argued with Hans, who at first was impressed by Hitler and his ideas of German national and racial superiority.

In Ulm, Hans belonged to a Hitler Youth group led by a man who had once belonged to more liberal youth organizations. In 1935, this man renounced those liberal values and dissolved the cell he had started in Ulm. But Hans had already been influenced by the character of the Ulm group, which was less authoritarian than other chapters of the Hitler Youth. He and some friends secretly continued some of their former activities, while still being active in the Hitler Youth.

A CHANGE OF HEART

A turning point for Hans came in 1936, when he took part in a large Nazi Party rally in Nuremberg. He had been selected to carry the Hitler Youth flag of Ulm. Many participants were thrilled by the Nuremberg rally, which had been choreographed by Hitler as a spectacular show and display of oratory, pageantry, and flag waving. He returned home deeply disappointed in the shallowness of the movement, with its constant military drills and lack of real contact between people.

From this time, Hans's commitment turned more decidedly toward the secret group, which—in addition to offering camping and hiking trips for boys—encouraged

It was after participating in a Nazi rally at Nuremberg, like the one seen here, that Hans Scholl started to become disillusioned with the Nazi regime.

members to explore other cultures, nature, and literature, including books that the Nazi minister of propaganda, Josef Goebbels, had burned as "degenerate" in 1933.

Meanwhile, Sophie was still in the Hitler group for girls. She enjoyed the camping, hiking, and bonfires. She found the friendships more important than the political work. So when her Jewish friends were not allowed to join, she did not understand why. She maintained her friendships with her Jewish friends, even though such relationships were now forbidden.

Sophie once wrote in a letter, "In school they told us that a German's attitude to his country is deliberately subjective and partisan. Unless it is deliberately objective, impartial, and evenhanded, I can't accept it."

In March 1937, Hans finished his elementary education. He then had to serve for two years in an army cavalry unit in Bad Cannstatt. But that fall, he was arrested and taken from his barracks to a jail in Stuttgart. It was part of a Nazi government crackdown on the d.j.1.11 organization. The Gestapo, or secret police, arrested young people whom they believed were involved. Four of the five Scholl children were arrested that November and taken to prison in Stuttgart. Sophie was released quickly, but Inge and Werner were kept in jail for a week and interrogated before being released. Hans himself was held in custody for five weeks before his commanding officer managed to have him released.

According to family and friends who remembered those days, the arrests were a turning point for the Scholl siblings in their view toward National Socialism. They now began to see that the Nazi dictatorship was trying to control all aspects of their lives.

In the spring of 1939, Hans began to study medicine at the university in Munich. Like the other medical students, he was a member of the Student Corps. This corps was a part of the army. Its members studied like other students, but during their vacations they had to do military service.

Not all of the young men in the military corps were true believers in Nazism. In fact, Hans made friends with a group of corpsmen who, like himself, were critical of the regime. He began to study religion and philosophy, and his feelings against National Socialism began to harden. He and his companions would discuss literature and art. They found they all respected some of the same ideals: individual freedom and responsibility.

World War II began on September 1, 1939, with the German invasion of Poland. In short order, Great Britain and France then declared war on Germany. The Nazis invaded France the following May and occupied Paris, the French capital, by mid-June of 1940. In June of 1941, Germany attacked the Soviet Union, and the war escalated to another level.

With this new stage, Hitler's plans now entered their most destructive phase. Accompanying the

While he was doing his medical studies, Hans met other students who were critical of National Socialist policies, which helped shape his views.

German forces across Poland and into the Soviet Union were special forces known as the Einsatzgruppen. Their mission: to find and isolate those despised groups the Nazis had selected, especially Jews, and kill them. Initially, these killings were done at mass shootings, with burials in mass graves.

NEW CONTACTS

In January 1942, Hitler's top officials met at Wannsee, a suburb of Berlin, the German capital. At the Wannsee conference, which lasted just eighty-five minutes, the upper echelons of the Nazi Party and government coordinated what was referred to as the *Endlosung der Judenfrage* (the Final Solution of the "Jewish question"). The solution was the elimination—murder—of all Europe's Jews, beginning in Poland and the Soviet Union. With this began the operation of the infamous death camps, most of them on Polish soil, including Auschwitz, Belzec, Treblinka, Majdanek, and Sobibor, where several million Jews were killed in the gas chambers.

Shortly after the war began, Hans, who was still a member of the Student Corps, was sent to France as a medic. After a few months, he returned to Munich, where he continued his studies as a medical student and continued to develop private contacts with fellow students and sympathetic professors.

Like her brother, Sophie started questioning Nazi policies after meeting other critics and learning the truth behind the propaganda.

Like Hans, Sophie was interested in philosophy and theology. Through her family's liberal contacts, she met artists whose work had been deemed degenerate by the Nazis. Slowly, she began to build her own ideas of resistance to the Nazi dictatorship.

While the German forces were overrunning and occupying Poland, Sophie graduated from high school. She arranged to become an apprentice kindergarten teacher at the Frobel Seminary in Ulm. She hoped that this would spare her from the obligation to work for the state, as all high school graduates were required to do before going to college.

But after nearly a year of working with the children at the seminary, Sophie learned that she still had to do her service for the state. She spent six months in the labor service at the Krauchenwies labor camp near Sigmaringen, and another six in the war auxiliary service, teaching in a kindergarten in Blumberg.

In March 1942, Sophie was finally able to return to Ulm. Sophie then went to Munich to study biology and philosophy at the Ludwig Maximilian University of Munich, where Hans was studying medicine. She arrived there on May 9, 1942—her twenty-first birthday. She celebrated with Hans and some of his new friends, fellow medical students Christoph Probst, a married man with two children, Alexander Schmorell, Willi Graf, and George Wittenstein. The men were all about the same age as Hans, in their mid- to late twenties. Sophie didn't know it then, but it would be her last birthday.

CHAPTER THREE

THE BIRTH OF THE WHITE ROSE

As Sophie learned the evening of her birthday, as her new group of friends discussed various issues, they all shared many similar views on politics. The group expressed anger over Nazi human rights abuses occurring within Germany and discontent with Hitler and his regime. Many would later witness even more heinous abuses during their compulsory military service—crimes committed in the name of Germany that did not reflect the values and ideas they themselves knew to be right. This disgust would fuel the group's drive to take action against the brutal regime. So who were these young men who had the courage to resist the Nazis?

ALEXANDER SCHMORELL

Alexander Schmorell had been born in Russia in 1917. His father was of German ancestry and worked as a physician. His mother, who was Russian, died soon after his birth. Alexander was a talented athlete, artist, and musician. After the revolution in Russia in 1917, which resulted in the overthrow of the tsar and the ascension to power of the Bolshevik (Communist) Party, the family moved to Germany.

Even so, the family retained strong cultural ties to Russia. They spoke Russian at home, where the children were looked after by a Russian nurse maid.

Alexander Schmorell (*left*) speaks with Hans Scholl before leaving for the eastern front in 1942, where they worked as medics and saw firsthand Nazi abuses against innocents.

Alexander chafed at unjust authority and developed a deep hatred for the Nazi regime, which defined the Slavic peoples, including the Russians and Poles, as inferior to the Aryans. In Hitler's grand scheme, the Slavs of eastern Europe were destined to give way to make room for Germany's *Lebensraum*, or living space. The fortunate ones would be enslaved; the rest killed.

Of the members of the White Rose, George Wittenstein remembered Alexander as being "the most complex of all because he was torn between his Russian ancestry and his German ancestry. When they emigrated to Germany they brought along a Russian nanny, so he was really brought up with Russian belief and culture."

CHRISTOPH PROBST

Christoph Probst's parents had divorced when he was young, and his father remarried a Jewish woman who was persecuted by the Nazis. His father, who committed suicide in 1936, had been a close friend of several famous artists whose work the Nazis classified as degenerate, including Paul Klee and Emil Nolde. Like Hans Scholl, Christoph had to do military service before entering the university to study medicine. He and Herta Dohrn, whom he married in 1941, had three children together. The last was born just before Christoph's execution for his activities with the White Rose.

Christoph Probst poses with one of his three children. In order to protect his family, he did not even inform his wife of his role in the White Rose resistance.

WILLI GRAF

Willi Graf came from a devout Catholic family whose religious values led him to an early rejection of National Socialism. Unlike the Scholl children, Willi never joined the Hitler Youth, and he was active in liberal Catholic youth groups instead, such as the Gray Order, which he joined in 1934. Graf had even been jailed for a short time because of his involvement with the group. Willi served in the military through the summer of 1942.

GEORGE WITTENSTEIN

George Wittenstein said that his own feelings against the regime began to take form as early as June 30, 1934. This is when Hitler had his best friend and rival Ernst Röhm, the leader of the paramilitary organization known as the SA (*Sturmabteilungen,* which literally means "storm troopers") or Brownshirts, killed, along with the rest of the group's leadership. The SA had provided the shock troops of the Nazi movement, providing muscle for the Party and attacking its political enemies. June 30, 1934, the date when Röhm and many of the group's leaders were betrayed by Hitler and arrested or killed, went down in history as the "Night of the Long Knives."

"Then," Wittenstein said, "one knew what was going on." Even so, it was not easy for people critical of the Nazis to find each other. It was too dangerous

Threatened by the SA's increased power, Hitler had his once close friend, SA leader Ernst Röhm (*right*), executed along with others Hitler believed to be opponents of his regime.

to openly state one's opposition, with the possible penalty of being sentenced to time in a concentration camp.

"You had to keep everything secret," remembered Wittenstein. "You could not even trust your friends. I was in a movie theater once and during a news reel, when Hitler was speaking, someone must have made a remark. He was removed by the Gestapo. When we talked anything about politics at home, we would put a tea cozy over the phone so no one at home would hear. It was a great risk, of course. It would be weeks and months before you knew someone well enough that you could talk to them."

COMING TOGETHER

When these young men met in Munich, they had different feelings about the war. Hans still had feelings of nationalism and felt the desire to help free Germany from the shame it felt after World War I, although he confided to his diary that "Germany has deserved this yoke." Willi, who was shocked by what he saw while serving on the Russian front, was already disillusioned with the Nazi regime.

Students who found that they shared similar critical attitudes usually met outside the classroom. The students who formed the White Rose met as members of the student medical corps of the army. George Wittenstein introduced Hans Scholl to Alexander Schmorell and another student, Hubert Furtwaengler. He first met Hans through a mutual friend. Scholl, Schmorell, and Wittenstein were all medics in the same company.

In the spring of 1941, Schmorell invited Hans to join in some evenings of literary readings that he had organized with Christoph Probst. At first, there was little or no discussion of politics at these gatherings. Instead, the students talked about literature, philosophy, religion, and music, and drank wine

Members of the White Rose were able to steal some moments of normalcy, even in wartime, attending concerts and doing other youthful activities.

together late into the night. Soon they were also getting together to attend concerts and to go hiking and swimming.

The friends held regular evenings in Munich with writers, philosophers, and artists. They discussed their ideas with professors Carl Muth, in whose home Sophie Scholl rented a room, and Theodor Haecker. Over time, discussions about how citizens should act under a dictatorship took place with increasing frequency.

SS soldiers force German Jews to a concentration camp as onlookers stand by. As the war wore on, Jews and other persecuted groups from German-occupied territories were also sent to death camps.

THE WHITE ROSE FORMS

By May 1942, Hans Scholl and Alexander Schmorell had decided that some action had to be taken against the Nazi regime. By this point, the students had heard rumors about mass deportations and shootings. But they probably did not know the full extent of everything that was going on in the lands occupied by Germany—Greater Germany, as the Nazis referred to it.

By then, Jews in occupied territories were being deported in large numbers to the death camps. In Germany itself, more than 300,000 Jews had been forced into emigration. (In 1933, at the start of the Hitler regime, there were approximately 500,000 Jews in Germany. They made up 1 percent of the population.) By the spring of 1942, plans had been made to ship the remaining German Jews to the "east" for "special treatment," which meant extermination.

Count Clemens August von Galen was a Catholic bishop from Germany and an outspoken critic of the Nazi regime, especially its racist policies and T4 euthanasia program.

The war was not going so well for Germany. A year had passed since Germany had attacked the Soviet Union, and the series of stunningly quick victories that the German armed forces had first achieved had come to an end. For most Germans, it was hard to learn the truth about the war because it was strictly forbidden to listen to foreign radio broadcasts. Within Germany, official broadcasts were completely controlled by the Nazi Ministry of Propaganda. These stations told the people what the government wanted them to hear: that Germany was winning.

Meanwhile, some public dissent had arisen. In August 1941, Count Clemens August von Galen, the Catholic bishop of Muenster, delivered a sermon attacking the Nazi euthanasia program, which had begun in 1939. In his sermon, the bishop spoke about what he called each individual's "obligations of conscience," which he said required them to oppose the taking of innocent life, even if such opposition cost them their own life.

"They were the first gassings," Franz Mueller says about the euthanasia program the bishop had condemned. Mueller remembers that in September 1941, he helped a school friend in Ulm, Heinz Brenner, reprint and mail out two or three hundred copies of the sermon to people the young men thought would be sympathetic. Among the recipients were the Scholls, and Mueller believes Hans was inspired by the leaflet. "At last somebody has had the courage to speak out," Hans is supposed to have said upon reading the sermon.

T4 EUTHANASIA PROGRAM

The T4 Euthanasia Program started by the Nazis targeted the elderly and individuals—including children—who struggled with terminal illnesses, mental or physical disabilities, and psychological or emotional issues. In short, it was designed to eliminate those whom Hitler believed were "burdensome" to German society—or "life unworthy of living" as they were known to Nazis. The program effectively turned doctors into executioners, justifying the deaths of the innocents as "mercy killings."

The program was actually the first Nazi mass murder plan, having started two years before the Final Solution was enacted. It was supported by eugenicists—pseudoscientists who believed that they could improve the health of the human race by selecting the traits that should carry into future generations. Essentially they had the power to determine who was fit to procreate. The Nazis believed that exterminating those who were "unfit" would improve German racial purity.

Rather than evaluate patients or read their records, medical "experts" did a survey of patients at hospitals, psychiatric institutions, and other facilities and decided who would live or die. Those chosen for extermination were killed by various methods, including starvation, lethal injection, and gassing in chambers that were set up as showers. Six killing centers with gas chambers in Germany were used for this purpose.

The program officially ran from 1939 to 1941. After that, it continued in secret underground. Estimates place the number killed through the T4 Program at 200,000 or more. Some doctors refused to participate. The Catholic Church opposed the killings, and several Catholic priests, most notably Count Clemens August von Galen spoke out against them openly.

"It gives you insight," says Mueller, "about what happened with young Germans of fifteen to sixteen years old." He and some other boys met secretly with a Catholic priest in Ulm who "'poisoned' us with good ideas, very cautiously."

According to Mueller, the priest never said "one word against Hitler," but he managed to get the boys to question the Nazi ideals. "For example," Mueller recalls, the priest "said one day in 1941 that one member of our school got a very high medal for courage at the front somewhere. The priest asked, 'Is courage what Aristotle described: living for your killing instincts, joy in fight and killing?' He said, 'You can only be courageous if you fight for a value. And what are the values here?'"

The friends talked for hours. "We learned to discuss," says Mueller. "And in a dictatorship, discussion is not allowed. It was an enormous training in free thinking and free discussion, and in laughing about the Nazis' ridiculous spectacular public events, with flags and marching and singing. Suddenly we had another view of the Nazis. If you are influenced by such fundamentals, you start thinking on your own, for example, with what the Nazis called the 'Jewish question.'"

Although the Nazis falsely blamed all of Germany's problems on its Jewish population, Hans and his friends, Mueller says, knew that "all human beings are created by God. That was very clear for us . . . If you have this kind of influence, you get other eyes. You saw things that others didn't see because they didn't want to open their eyes."

Mueller and his friends wanted to do something against the dictatorship, and through their friends, the Scholls, they became involved in the White Rose. They knew it was risky. As Mueller's friend Heinz Brenner explained to him in a letter from the Russian front at the end of 1941: "We have a fifty-fifty chance to survive the Nazis and the war. On the other hand, there is a 50 percent chance we will be killed by being and acting against Hitler. It is no question that our death only makes sense if we are fighting against Hitler and not for him in Russia." Five months later, Mueller, too, was sent to the front. In the meantime, he became involved with the White Rose.

The students formed the White Rose movement in Munich in June of 1942. They decided to express their views in leaflets. The first goal of their campaign was to spread the word that there were Germans who were opposed to Hitler. They knew they could not overthrow the government, and they did not encourage a revolution. But they could spread information and encourage other Germans to question the dictatorship.

CHAPTER FOUR

TAKING ACTION

The White Rose was committed to passive resistance. The leaflets its members distributed made sure to make this clear. The leaflets were eloquent pleas to the German public and borrowed heavily from renowned thinkers and writers—including such celebrated German writers as Friedrich Schiller and Johann Wolfgang von Goethe—as well as Christian teachings to make their case.

THE FIRST LEAFLET

Hans Scholl and Alexander Schmorell prepared the first leaflet. It was distributed on June 6, 1942, under the title "Leaflets of the White Rose." It criticized Germans who passively accepted Hitler's regime and urged them to passively resist the Nazis instead. The leaflet begins:

> Nothing is less worthy of a civilized people than to let themselves be governed—without resistance—by an

irresponsible and base clique. Is not every honest German today ashamed of his government? And who among us can guess the dimensions of the shame that will engulf us and our children, when the veil falls from our eyes one day and the most gruesome and immeasurable crimes come to light?

-excerpt from the first leaflet

Flugblätter der Weissen Rose.

I

Nichts ist eines Kulturvolkes unwürdiger, als sich ohne Widerstand von einer verantwortungslosen und dunklen Trieben ergebenen Herrscherclique "regieren" zu lassen. Ist es nicht so, dass sich jeder ehrliche Deutsche heute seiner Regierung schämt, und wer von uns ahnt das Ausmass der Schmach, die über uns und unsere Kinder kommen wird, wenn einst der Schleier von unseren Augen gefallen ist und die grauenvollsten und jeglichen Mass unendlich überschreitenden Verbrechen ans Tageslicht treten? Wenn das deutsche Volk schon so in seinem tiefsten Wesen korrumpiert und zerfallen ist, dass es ohne eine Hand zu regen, im leichtsinnigen Vertrauen auf eine fragwürdige Gesetzmässigkeit der Geschichte, das Höchste, das ein Mensch besitzt, und das ihn über jede andere Kreatur erhöht, nämlich den freien Willen, preisgibt, die Freiheit des Menschen preisgibt, selbst mit einzugreifen in das Rad der Geschichte und es seiner vernünftigen Entscheidung unterzuordnen, wenn die Deutschen so jeder Individualität bar, schon so sehr zur geistlosen und feigen Masse geworden sind, dann, ja dann verdienen sie den Untergang.

Goethe spricht von den Deutschen als einem tragischen Volke, gleich dem der Juden und Griechen, aber heute hat es eher den Anschein, als sei es eine seichte, willenlose Herde von Mitläufern, denen das Mark aus dem Innersten gesogen und nun ihres Kernes beraubt, bereit sind sich in den Untergang hetzen zu lassen. Es scheint so - aber es ist nicht so; vielmehr hat man in langsamer, trügerischer, systematischer Vergewaltigung jeden einzelnen in ein geistiges Gefängnis gesteckt, und erst, als er darin gefesselt lag, wurde er sich des Verhängnisses bewusst. Wenige nur erkannten das drohende Verderben, und der Lohn für ihr heroisches Mahnen war der Tod. Ueber das Schicksal dieser Menschen wird noch zu reden sein.

Wenn jeder wartet, bis der Andere anfängt, werden die Boten der rächenden Nemesis unaufhaltsam näher und näher rücken, dann wird auch das letzte Opfer sinnlos in den Rachen des unersättlichen Dämons geworfen sein. Daher muss jeder Einzelne seiner Verantwortung als Mitglied der christlichen und abendländischen Kultur bewusst in dieser letzten Stunde sich wehren so viel er kann, arbeiten wider die Geisel der Menschheit, wider den Faschismus und jedes ihm ähnliche System des absoluten Staates. Leistet passiven Widerstand - Widerstand - wo immer Ihr auch seid, verhindert das Weiterlaufen dieser atheistischen Kriegsmaschine, ehe es zu spät ist, ehe die letzten Städte ein Trümmerhaufen sind, gleich Köln, und ehe die letzte Jugend des Volkes irgendwo für die Hybris eines Untermenschen verblutet ist. Vergesst nicht, dass ein jedes Volk diejenige Regierung verdient, die es erträgt!

Aus Friedrich Schiller, "Die Gesetzgebung des Lykurgus und Solon":

"....Gegen seinen eigenen Zweck gehalten, ist die Gesetzgebung des Lykurgus ein Meisterstück der Staats- und Menschenkunde. Er wollte einen mächtigen, in sich selbst gegründeten, unzerstörbaren Staat; politische Stärke und Dauerhaftigkeit waren das Ziel, wonach er strebte, und dieses Ziel hat er so weit erreicht, als unter seinen Umständen möglich war. Aber hält man den Zweck, welchen Lykurgus sich vorsetzte, gegen den Zweck der Menschheit, so muss eine tiefe Missbilligung an die Stelle der Bewunderung treten, die uns der erste, flüchtige Blick abgewon n hat. Alles darf dem Besten des Staates zum Opfer gebracht werden, nur dasjenige nicht, dem der Staat selbst nur als ein Mittel dient. Der Staat selbst ist niemals Zweck, er ist nur wichtig als eine Bedingung, unter welcher der Zweck der Menschheit erfüllt werden kann, und dieser Zweck der Menschheit ist kein anderer, als Ausbildung aller Kräfte des Menschen, Fortschreitung. Hindert eine Staatsverfassung, dass alle Kräfte, die im Menschen liegen, sich entwickeln; hindert sie die Fortschreitung des Geistes, so ist sie verwerflich und schädlich, sie mag übrigens noch so durchdacht und in ihrer Art noch so vollkommen sein. Ihre Dauerhaftigkeit selbst gereicht ihr alsdann vielmehr zum Vorwurf, als zum Ruhme - sie ist dann nur ein verlängertes Uebel; je länger sie Bestand hat, umso schädlicher ist sie.

.....Auf Unkosten aller sittlichen Gefühle wurde das politische Verdienst errungen und die Fähigkeit dazu ausgebildet. In Sparta gab es keine eheliche Liebe, keine Mutterliebe, keine kindliche Liebe, keine Freundschaft - es gab nichts als Bürger, nichts als bürgerliche Tugend. ....Ein Staatsgesetz machte den Spartanern die Unmenschlichkeit gegen ihre Sklaven zur Pflicht; in diesen unglücklichen Schlachtopfern wurde die Menschheit beschimpft und misshandelt. In dem spartanischen Gesetzbuche selbst wurde der gefährliche Grundsatz gepredigt, Menschen als Mittel und Zweck zu betrachten - dadurch wurden die Grundfesten des Naturrechts und der Sittlichkeit gesetzmässig eingerissen. .....Welch schöneres Schauspiel gibt der rauhe Krieger Cajus Marcius in seinem Lager vor Rom, der Rache und Sieg aufopfert, weil er die Tränen der Mutter nicht fliessen sehen kann!"

"...Der Staat (des Lykurgus) könnte nur unter der einzigen Bedingung fortdauern, wenn der Geist des Volks stillestünde; er könnte sich also nur dadurch erhalten, dass er den höchsten und einzigen Zweck eines Staates verfehlte."

Aus Goethe "Des Epimenides Erwachen", zweiter Aufzug, vierter Auftritt:

Genien

.....
Doch was den Abgrund kühn entstiegen,
Kann durch ein ehernes Geschick
Den halben Weltkreis überstiegen,
Zum Abgrund muss es doch zurück.
Schon droht ein ungeheures Bangen,
Vergebens wird er widerstehn!
Und alle, die noch an ihn hangen,
Sie müssen mit zu Grunde gehn.

Hoffnung

Nun begegn' ich meinen Braven,
Die sich in der Nacht versammelt,
Um zu schweigen, nicht zu schlafen,
Und das schöne Wort der Freiheit
Wird gelispelt und gestammelt,
Bis in ungewohnter Neuheit
Wir an unsrer Tempel Stufen
Wieder neu entzückt es rufen:
(Mit Ueberzeugung, laut:)
Freiheit!
(gemässigter)
Freiheit!
(von allen Seiten und Enden Echo:)
Freiheit!

Wir bitten Sie, dieses Blatt mit möglichst vielen Durchschlägen abzuschreiben und weiter zu verteilen!

Hans Scholl and Alexander Schmorell were the primary authors of the first five leaflets, although Sophie and Christoph probably also contributed. More members were involved in distributing the leaflets.

Less than a year later, after he had been arrested and was being interrogated by the Gestapo, Hans said that as a German citizen he felt a duty to act against the government that was committing crimes against people in occupied countries. He wanted to reach the academic community, whom he believed had a greater responsibility to inspire others or challenge them out of their complacency. He believed it was important to shorten the war so Europe could be rebuilt and Germany could become a democracy. He said he had acted as a citizen of the state who was concerned with its fate.

The first leaflet, as well as future ones, closed with the words, "We ask you to please make as many copies of this leaflet as possible and pass it on." The first leaflet was distributed only a few weeks after Sophie began her university studies in Munich. At first, Sophie was not sure who was involved. When she learned the truth, she wanted to help. Initially, Hans did not want young women to take part in the risky work. But eventually, Sophie helped prepare and distribute the leaflets. She also managed the group's finances.

"Sophie Scholl, she was the heart—and Hans and Alex were the thinking behind the White Rose," says Franz Mueller, who became involved in disseminating the leaflets in Ulm, in the summer of 1942, after he had already done some military service in France. "I got the news of the White Rose on the first or second of July," he recalls. He had seen some of Hans Scholl's writing already, and "thought he must have written the leaflet."

Another copy was sent to the family of the landlord where Traute LaFrenz was living. Like Sophie and Franz, Traute was not sure at first who was responsible. But when she read the various quotes from philosophers contained in the leaflet, she felt sure it must have come from her friends. She told Hermann Vinke that in the second leaflet she saw a "verse from Ecclesiastes that I had once given to Hans. Now I knew. I asked Hans about it. He said it was wrong to ask the author, that the number of immediate coworkers must be kept to a minimum, and that the less I knew the better for me." Traute ended up helping to distribute the leaflets.

GAINING MOMENTUM

That summer, before being sent to the Russian front with the Student Corps, the friends prepared three more leaflets bearing the title, "Leaflets of the White Rose." Christoph added to what Hans and Alex had written. It is not clear that Willi was involved until late summer. The leaflets were all mailed between mid-June and mid-July of 1942. By then, about a dozen friends were involved in one way or another.

The leaflets were duplicated on hand-operated mimeograph machines and sent to the addresses of possible sympathizers. The machines, paper, ink, and stamps had to be procured in secrecy. Anyone buying a lot of stamps, for example, might be suspected of treason. Alex had bought the typewriter, duplicating machine, stencils, and paper with his allowance money. Architect Manfred Eickemeyer let the students use his studio for the printing.

A few hundred copies of each leaflet were printed at first. More were printed later. Some were mailed to addresses taken from phone books, others to specific individuals at various universities. Recipients also included owners of pubs. Some leaflets were placed in public telephones.

The second leaflet was even more explicit than the first. It referred directly to the murder of "three hundred thousand Jews" and intellectuals in occupied Poland, forcing readers to confront information that the Nazi government would rather they not know.

Now is the time for us to come together again, to enlighten each other, to keep our purpose in mind and give ourselves no rest until the last person is convinced of the urgency of the struggle against this system. If this creates a wave of unrest through the land, if "it is in the air," then with a final tremendous effort this system can be shaken off. An end to the terror is always better than terror without an end.

—excerpt from the second leaflet

"Nobody believed what was written about the mass killing," says Mueller. "I think even Jewish people didn't believe it. This was one of the first groups that announced it."

"The government tried to keep this a secret but we knew because a friend of ours had seen it in Russia," said Wittenstein. "He saw shootings and the camps . . . and the chimneys of the crematoria in the concentration camps. He came home on furlough for a couple of weeks and told us. He was shocked."

Before he was sent off to military auxiliary service in Alsace in late July, Mueller and a friend in Ulm helped prepare leaflets for Sophie Scholl to distribute. "There were about 1,000, 1,200, in envelopes. I gave addresses to my friend and he typed it," Mueller says. They worked secretly behind the organ in the Martin Luther Church in Ulm.

The third leaflet called on Germans to commit sabotage against the German war industry. It also proposed an alternative to the Nazi government—a government that would place the protection of the individual and the community above all else. The fourth leaflet, which Hans composed himself, focused on an explanation of the war as an expression of evil.

All the leaflets attacked the Nazi regime and enumerated its crimes, from the mass extermination of Jews and the murder of the Polish nobility and intellectual elite to the dictatorship and the elimination of the personal freedom of the German people. They contained quotes from great philosophers and writers, including Goethe, Aristotle, and Lao-tzu.

> We want to try to show you that everyone is able to do something to help destroy this system . . . Sabotage in armaments plants and war industries, sabotage at public gatherings, rallies, ceremonies, and organizations of the National Socialist Party . . . Sabotage in all areas of science and scholarship that advance the war effort . . . Sabotage in all cultural institutions that could enhance the "prestige" of the fascists . . . Sabotage in all writing, all newspapers that support the "government" and spread the brown lie. Don't waste a single penny at public drives (even if they are under the disguise of charitable organizations). In reality the proceeds do not help the Red Cross or the needy.

> —excerpt from the third leaflet

People were afraid to be caught with the leaflets, and many recipients turned them in to the Gestapo, which began to investigate their origin. The secret police were able to tap telephones and censor mail. By late summer, the police were fairly sure that the leaflets were being produced in Munich and were somehow associated with the university.

The police frequently searched luggage on trains, so students transporting the leaflets had to be extremely careful. Often, they would place the suitcase containing leaflets in another car of the train and then sit elsewhere. When the train would arrive at the destination, the students would retrieve the leaflets. Often, the girls took on this work as they believed they were less likely to be searched by the police.

In July, after the first four leaflets were distributed, Hans, Alexander, Hubert Furtwaengler (who

The female members of the White Rose were instrumental in transporting leaflets by train. They believed they were less likely to get caught by Nazi officials, who had a significant presence at train stations.

knew about the White Rose but did not participate), George, and Willi were sent to the eastern front, to work as medics. They left Munich on July 23, 1942. They remained there until October. On the evening before their departure for Russia, the friends met to discuss how to continue their activities. They decided to seek new partners for the resistance and had to think about which of their friends could be trusted.

During this short tour of duty in the occupied Soviet Union, the young men saw the beauty of the countryside and got to know some Russians. But they also saw abuses being committed by the German military against innocent people. Seeing these things left a deep impression on them and further convinced them that they were right to encourage resistance. Wittenstein characterized their reaction to what they saw as "shock and horror and rage."

Neither Hitler nor Goebbels has counted the dead. Every day, thousands die in Russia. It is the harvest time and the reaper cuts the ripe grain with broader strokes. Mourning moved into the cottages of the land, and no one is there who dries the tears of the mother. Hitler gives lies in return to those whose dearest belongings have been stolen and who have been driven into a meaningless death.

Every word that comes out of Hitler's mouth is a lie. If he says peace he means war, and if he in his outrageous way uses the name of the Almighty, he means the power of evil, the fallen angel, Satan. We have to fight against the evil, where it is at its most powerful, and it is most powerful in the might of Hitler.

—excerpt from the fourth leaflet

While her brother and his friends were in Russia, Sophie left Munich for the summer break, returning to Ulm. During her two-month vacation, Sophie had to work in an armaments factory in Ulm, where she worked alongside slave laborers from the Soviet Union. All students who were not on the front had to do armaments work. Her younger brother, Werner, was also in Russia at this time.

That summer, Robert Scholl had been arrested for making critical remarks about Hitler. He made the remarks in his own office, and a secretary who overheard him reported him to the Gestapo. In August 1942, he was convicted of "malicious slander of the Führer" and was sentenced to prison for four months. When he was released, he was not permitted to work at his old job.

That summer, Sophie was shocked to learn from a friend that for months the SS had been removing mentally disabled children from hospitals and killing them in gas chambers. Sophie returned to Munich in October, at about the same time that her brother and his friends returned from Russia.

Now, even more than ever, they were convinced that resistance was essential. They collected money from friends for paper and new equipment. Traute got a new mimeograph machine from her uncle's office equipment store in Vienna, the capital of Austria. Sophie bought stencils and paper in stores around Munich.

That fall, Alex and Hans made contact with Falk Harnack, who was involved in a resistance group that worked within the Nazi government. The White Rose students were eager to make contact with the members of this resistance group, some of whose members were reputedly close to Hitler in Berlin. Reportedly, Harnack informed them there was a plan in the works for an attack on Hitler.

In the meantime, Christoph had been trans-

After being acquitted for his involvement with the White Rose, Falk Harnack (*left*) went on to be a film director and screenwriter. Some of his works were about German resistance to the Nazis.

ferred to Innsbruck, Austria, in December 1942 and had less contact with the group. This left Hans and Sophie to make most of the decisions for the group. By then, the siblings were living in adjacent rooms in an apartment on Franz Josef Street, and the other students began to meet there. As always, the conspirators were careful to hide their activities from outsiders, including their families.

"No family knew. Not one," says Franz Mueller. "We had to lie to our parents when they would ask, 'Where are you coming from in the night?' It was always in the back of our minds that they could arrest our families. My father had a heart attack when he heard I was arrested." That arrest took place in February 1943.

"No member of any family knew of what we were doing," agreed Wittenstein, "because we had to protect them. We all were aware that we were risking our necks."

Meanwhile, members of the group distributed leaflets to larger cities in the south of Germany, including Freiburg, Stuttgart, and Karlsruhe. Hans Hirzel took stacks of leaflets to Stuttgart. In November and December, Traute LaFrenz brought copies to her friend, Heinz Kucharski who was active with an opposition group in Hamburg. Later, Kucharski would be sentenced to death for his activities, but he would escape at the last minute.

In January, the five core members of the White Rose—Hans, Sophie, Alex, Christoph, and Willi— decided to talk about their resistance work with their philosophy professor, Kurt Huber. He agreed to help and support them. He wrote the sixth, and last, leaflet himself.

Huber's resistance to the regime had developed slowly. He chafed at the antireligious position of the Nazis. When he learned about the atrocities being committed during the war, he became vehemently opposed to the regime. He managed to criticize the government during his lectures on philosophy, without actually saying anything concrete against it. Like the students, he was in favor of protecting the rights of individuals—something that the totalitarian system did not do.

SPREADING THE WORD

By January 1943, the White Rose had expanded its contacts around the country and realized their views were shared by others. In February, Hans's new girlfriend, Gisela Schertling, was let in on what the White Rose group was doing.

The last two leaflets of the White Rose were printed in January and February 1943, under the title "Leaflets of the Resistance." These last leaflets were produced in much greater numbers than the first four. Using their new, larger mimeograph machine, working day and night, they printed more than 8,000 copies. Sophie and Traute bought the paper and stamps in different places around Munich to avoid arousing suspicion. The

AN INFAMOUS SPEECH

Early in January 1943, something occurred that helped convince the White Rose activists that they had more supporters in Germany. On January 13, the Nazi gauleiter, or district leader of, Munich, Paul Giesler, made a speech on the 470th anniversary of the university. He told the students in an assembly that women should not be studying. Instead, they should be making babies for Germany. Furthermore, he said he would provide his own adjutants as husbands for those girls who could not attract a man on their own.

When they heard this, several young women were so insulted that they stood up and walked out of the hall. They were arrested. Then the young men in the hall protested. They beat up the Nazi student leader and would not let him go until the women were released. A few days later, Giesler spoke again at the university and apologized. This may have shown the students that their protest had an effect. This anti-Nazi demonstration gave encouragement to the White Rose, but it also prompted the Gestapo to look harder for dissidents. The danger was increasing for members of the resistance.

Paul Giesler was a ruthless and loyal follower of Hitler. He was instrumental in the arrests of the White Rose members in 1943.

students took stimulants to stay awake. This may have affected their judgment later on, in a tragic way.

The fifth leaflet was a collaborative effort of Hans and Alex. It was brief and offered a plan for Germany's future.

A Call to All Germans!
It is mathematically certain that Hitler is leading the German people into an abyss. Hitler cannot win the war; he can only prolong it! His guilt and that of his helpers has overstepped all bounds. Retribution is slipping closer and closer!
. . . Germans! Do you and your children want to suffer the same fate as the Jews? Freedom of speech, freedom of religion, protection of individuals from the arbitrary will of a violent, criminal state, this will be the foundation for a new Europe!

—excerpt from the fifth leaflet

The conspirators carried the pamphlets to different places around the country in suitcases and mailed them from different places in order to make it seem like the White Rose movement was bigger than it was. Some leaflets were left in public places at night, while others were placed on parked cars. Later, Sophie's sister, Elisabeth, would recall her saying that "the night is a friend of the free." Franz

German soldiers crouch near anti-tank guns during the Battle of Stalingrad. The battle, which lasted from July 1942 until February 1943, was a critical win for the Allied forces.

Mueller, Hans Hirzel, and his sister Suzanne mailed leaflets from Ulm.

THE BATTLE OF STALINGRAD

In early February 1943, the German forces suffered their final defeat in Stalingrad. This was a true turning point in the war.

EIN DEUTSCHES FLUGBLATT

DIES ist der Text eines deutschen Flugblatts, von dem ein Exemplar nach England gelangt ist. Studenten der Universität München haben es im Februar dieses Jahres verfasst und in der Universität verteilt. Sechs von ihnen sind dafür hingerichtet worden, andere wurden eingesperrt, andere strafweise an die Front geschickt. Seither werden auch an allen anderen deutschen Universitäten die Studenten „ausgesiebt". Das Flugblatt drückt also offenbar die Gesinnungen eines beträchtlichen Teils der deutschen Studenten aus.

Aber es sind nicht nur die Studenten. In allen Schichten gibt es Deutsche, die Deutschlands wirkliche Lage erkannt haben ; Goebbels schimpft sie „die Objektiven". Ob Deutschland noch selber sein Schicksai wenden kann, hängt davon ab, dass diese Menschen sich zusammenfinden und handeln. Das weiss Goebbels, und deswegen beteuert er krampfhaft, „dass diese Sorte Mensch zahlenmässig nicht ins Gewicht fällt". Sie sollen nicht wissen, wie viele sie sind.

Wir werden den Krieg sowieso gewinnen. Aber wir sehen nicht ein, warum die Vernünftigen und Anständigen in Deutschland nicht zu Worte kommen sollen. Deswegen werfen die Flieger der RAF zugleich mit ihren Bomben jetzt dieses Flugblatt, für das sechs junge Deutsche gestorben sind, und das die Gestapo natürlich sofort konfisziert hat, in Millionen von Exemplaren über Deutschland ab.

Manifest der Münchner Studenten

Erschüttert steht unser Volk vor dem Untergang der Männer von Stalingrad. 330.000 deutsche Männer hat die geniale Strategie des Weltkriegsgefreiten sinn- und verantwortungslos in Tod und Derberben gehetzt. Führer, wir danken Dir !

Es gärt im deutschen Volk. Wollen wir weiter einem Dilettanten das Schicksal unserer Armeen anvertrauen ? Wollen wir den niedrigsten Machtinstinkten einer Parteiclique den Rest der deutschen Jugend opfern ? Nimmermehr!

Der Tag der Abrechnung ist gekommen, der Abrechnung unserer deutschen Jugend mit der verabscheuungswürdigsten Tyrannei, die unser Volk je erduldet hat. Im Namen des ganzen deutschen Volkes fordern wir von dem Staat Adolf Hitlers die persönliche Freiheit, das kostbarste Gut der Deutschen zurück, um das er uns in der erbärmlichsten Weise betrogen hat.

In einem Staat rücksichtsloser Knebelung jeder freien Meinungsäusserung sind wir aufgewachsen.

G.39

Manifes

H.J., SA und S... fruchtbarsten Bi... Lebens zu unif... tionieren, zu n... Weltanschaulich... verächtliche M... mende Selbstd... werten in einem... zu ersticken. Ein... sie teuflischer u... nicht gedacht we... künftigen Parte... burgen zu gottl... gewissenlosen A... buben heran, 3... Führergefolgsch... des Geistes" ... dieser neuen... Knüppel zu ma...

Stoßtrupfer... dentenführern... ...anten wie Schu... Gauleiter greife... den Studentin... Deutsche Studen... Münchner Hoch... lung ihrer Ehre... wort gegeben... haben sich für... eingesetzt und... ist ein Anfang... unserer freien... ohne die geistige... fen werden könn... den tapferen K... Kameraden, die... Beispiel vorang...

Es gibt für u... Kampf gegen d... aus den Parl... denen man u... mundtot macher... den Hörsälen ľ... Oberführer und... geht uns um wa... echte Geistesfre...

The sixth leaflet, written by Kurt Huber, is remembered particularly for its powerful and clever language. It appealed to Germans to open their eyes to Nazi policies after the Battle of Stalingrad.

ünchner Studenten
tſetzung

mittel kann uns ſchrecken, auch nicht
die Schließung unſerer Hochſchulen.
Es gilt den Kampf jedes einzelnen
von uns um unſere Zukunft,
unſere Freiheit und Ehre in einem
ſeiner ſittlichen Verantwortung be-
wußten Staatsweſen.

Freiheit und Ehre ! Zehn Jahre
lang haben Hitler und ſeine Genoſſen
die beiden herrlichen deutſchen Worte
bis zum Ekel ausgequetſcht, abge-
droſchen, verdreht, wie es nur
Dilettanten vermögen, die die höch-
ſten Werte einer Nation vor die Säue
werfen. Was ihnen Freiheit und
Ehre gilt, das haben ſie in zehn
Jahren der Zerſtörung aller materiel-
len und geiſtigen Freiheit, aller ſittlichen Subſtanz im deutſchen Volk
genugſam gezeigt. Auch dem dümm-
ſten Deutſchen hat das furchtbare
Blutbad die Augen geöffnet, das
ſie im Namen von Freiheit und Ehre
der deutſchen Nation in ganz Europa
angerichtet haben und täglich neu
anrichten. Der deutſche Name bleibt
für immer geſchändet, wenn nicht
die deutſche Jugend endlich aufſteht,
rächt und ſühnt zugleich, ſeine
Peiniger zerſchmettert und ein neues,
geiſtiges Europa aufrichtet.

Studentinnen! Studenten! Auf
uns ſieht das deutſche Volk. Von uns
erwartet es, ſo wie in 1813 die
Brechung des napoleoniſchen, ſo
1943 des nationalſozialiſtiſchen
Terrors aus der Macht des Geiſtes.
Bereſina und Stalingrad flammen im
Oſten auf, die Toten von Stalingrad
beſchwören uns : Friſch auf, mein
Volk, die Flammenzeichen rauchen!

Unſer Volk ſteht im Aufbruch
gegen die Verknechtung Europas
durch den Nationalſozialismus, im
neuen gläubigen Durchbruch von
Freiheit und Ehre!

"After Stalingrad, who could speak of victory, of 'the Führer knows all?'" asks Mueller. "It was so stupid and terrible. After Stalingrad, Germans didn't trust themselves as before. Some doubts were coming up."

The sixth leaflet was written by Kurt Huber in response to the German defeat at Stalingrad. The students made more than 2,000 copies on February 12 and mailed about 1,000 of them on the 15th. The leaflet was aimed at students and lambasted Hitler for leading Germany into the tragedy of Stalingrad. The sixth leaflet was also brought to England by Helmuth von Moltke (a German jurist who belonged to another resistance movement), and copies were thrown out of British airplanes flying over Germany.

Kurt Huber taught Hans Scholl and Alexander Schmorell before joining the White Rose. The leaflet he authored would be the final one to be circulated.

Shaken, our people behold the loss of
the men of Stalingrad. Three hundred and
thirty thousand German men were sent,
senselessly and irresponsibly, to their death
and destruction by the ingenious strate-
gies of the World War I Private First Class.
Führer, we thank you!

...For us, there is only one slogan:
Struggle against the party! Quit the party
organizations that keep us politically dumb!
Quit the lecture halls of the SS corporals
and sergeants and party grovelers. We want
true learning and real spiritual freedom.

—excerpt from the sixth leaflet

Right after the defeat at Stalingrad—on
three days in early February—Hans, Alex, and Willi
painted graffiti with tar-based paint on buildings
in Munich: slogans such as "Down with Hitler!"
"Freedom!" and "Hitler Mass Murderer," along with
crossed-out swastikas. Sophie wanted to take part
but the men would not let her. They knew that the
streets were being patrolled by police. In fact, the
newspapers reported that on February 4 the police
had carried out a major search throughout Munich
for those responsible for the graffiti and leaflets.

On February 5, the public prosecutor for the
city of Munich reported to the Supreme Court about
"subversive activities in Munich." The report stated
that "the perpetrators are unknown. The house-

holders have been ordered to remove the slogans."
The report also noted that, in recent days, approximately 1,300 anti-Nazi leaflets had been found in
the streets. Again, the perpetrators were unknown.

Even others in the White Rose, including
Traute LaFrenz, did not realize that the group was
responsible for the graffiti. "I never knew to the
very end that they were the only ones. I don't
know if Hans made me believe that, or if I just
could not think that four or five people could do all
that." They had hit twenty-nine sites in just a few
nights. She assumed another organization must
have done it. She only later discovered the truth.

CHAPTER FIVE

THE WHITE ROSE ON TRIAL

With increased visibility came increased danger for the White Rose. The Gestapo had already launched an investigation after the first leaflets had been distributed in 1942. With its characteristic ruthlessness, the Gestapo intensified the investigation after the mailing of the fifth leaflet on January 28. The Gestapo reasoned that the leaflets had made their way around the country on trains. Thus, starting in February, train searches in several cities became common. Ads in southern German newspapers tried to recruit citizens into the search, asking for tips. A reward of 1,000 reichsmarks was offered to anyone who helped in locating members of the resistance. After the printing of the sixth—and last—leaflet in February 1943, the Gestapo succeeded in its search.

THE ARRESTS

"They arrested Hans Hirzel first, on the 14th or 15th of February," says Mueller. "He had been denounced by Hitler Youth leaders. During the interrogation by the Gestapo in Ulm, they asked if he knew Sophie Scholl. When he came out of the Gestapo in Ulm, he saw that no one was following him, and he went to the Scholls. He did not call. He was the first to warn the Scholls. But Inge did not take it so seriously. She thought he was making up stories. He said, 'You have to phone immediately' to tell Hans that the police were on his trail."

Otl Aichler, Inge's boyfriend, called Hans on February 17 and told him he had important news. They planned to meet at eleven the following morning. But it would be too late. That morning, Hans and Sophie had carried a suitcase of leaflets to the university. While students were in class, Hans and Sophie placed piles of Huber's final leaflet in the halls. They wanted to finish before the students came out of class, so they ran outside. But when they realized there were still leaflets in the suitcase, they returned to the hall. From an upper balcony, Sophie threw the remaining leaflets out onto the courtyard below. Sophie later told the Gestapo that it was either high spirits or stupidity that made her throw eighty to one hundred leaflets from the third floor of the university into the inner courtyard.

They had been observed by university custodian Jakob Schmidt who reported them to the Gestapo. The university doors were locked and all the students who had picked up leaflets had to turn them over. Hans and Sophie were brought to the office of the president, SS *Obersturmführer* Dr. Walter Wuest, a professor of so-called Aryan language and culture. They were interrogated by Robert Mohr of the Gestapo. Mohr had the police gather all the leaflets. They fit exactly into the empty suitcases that Hans and Sophie were carrying. The siblings were arrested and taken to Gestapo Headquarters at Wittelsbach Palace. Their rooms at Franz Josef Street were searched, and the police found hundreds of unused stamps.

Willi Graf, who had not heard about the arrests, was picked up that day after he returned home from working at the university hospital. Alexander Schmorell was warned by his mother, and he stayed with a friend that night who was not part of the White Rose.

When he was arrested, Hans had a handwritten rough draft of a leaflet by Christoph Probst in his pocket. Though Hans tried to destroy it, the police were able to identify Christoph's handwriting through papers they found in Hans's room. Christoph, who was in Innsbruck and unaware of these developments, was arrested the next day. His wife had just given birth to their third child.

At Wittelsbach, Hans and Sophie were interrogated separately for seventeen hours. They could no longer deny their involvement after the evidence was found in their apartment. They each said that only the two of them were responsible for the

Roland Freisler was a hard-line Nazi judge who employed tactics such as bullying and shouting at defendants—especially those seen as threats to the Nazi Party—during a trial.

White Rose movement. They were each placed in a cell with another political prisoner. The interrogation continued for four days.

Hans, Sophie, and Christoph received court-appointed lawyers. The trial was set for the following Monday, February 22. For the trial, the notoriously harsh Nazi judge Roland Freisler, president of the People's Court, came to Munich from Berlin. This was meant to send a message to the public—even though Germany was already being bombed by the Allies, it was still urgent to stifle opposition to the war and the Nazi Party.

In her cell, Sophie asked her lawyer if her brother would be executed by firing squad, since he had been part of the army and on the front and he deserved that honor. The lawyer did not answer. She then asked if she was to be hanged or beheaded. Again, she received no answer.

THE FIRST TRIAL

Robert and Magdalene Scholl found out from George Wittenstein on Friday the 19th about the arrests. On Monday, the 22nd, they went to Munich to try to get into the trial. The trial, which would last from 9 AM to 1 PM, was like a public event, and tickets had been given only to loyal Party members. Still, the Scholls managed to sneak in. Robert Scholl tried to speak for his children during the trial, but then he and Magdalene were thrown out and not permitted to return to the courtroom.

Sophie's words during the trial would later become famous. She told Judge Freisler that what they had done was simply to express "what many people are thinking. They just don't dare say it out loud!" She also told him that "everyone knows" that Germany had already lost the war. "Why are you so cowardly as to not recognize that?"

Hans and Sophie tried to take all the blame so that their friend Christoph could go free. But Freisler interrupted Hans during the trial and told him that if he had nothing to say for himself, then he should remain silent.

All were found guilty of high treason and

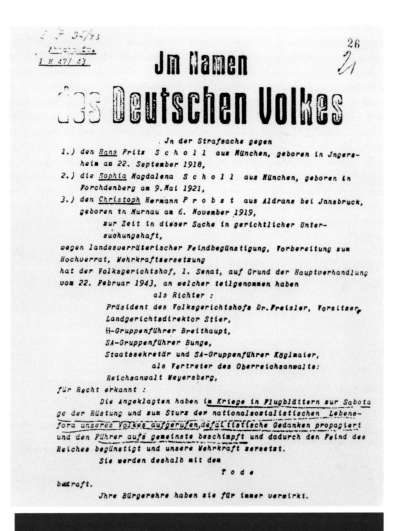

sentenced to death by guillotine. They were taken
from the court to Stadelheim Prison immediately
after the verdict was announced. The only one to

Copies of the sentences against White Rose members are now on display at a memorial established in the court in which they were tried.

make a last statement, Christoph asked to be pardoned because of his three children and ill wife. His plea did not work.

FINAL MOMENTS

At Stadelheim, the guards allowed Hans and Sophie separately to see their parents. Robert told Hans that he would be famous for what he had done. Hans, who was wearing a prison uniform, asked his parents to say farewell to his friends. He thanked his parents for the years he had had with them and cried when he mentioned the name of one friend. Sophie, who was wearing her own clothes, smiled and accepted some cakes from her mother, saying that she had not had lunch. Her mother said, "I'll never see you come through the door again." Sophie responded that it would only be a few years of life that she would miss. But she was worried about how her mother would take the deaths of two children.

Christoph was not allowed to meet his family. He spoke instead with a priest and was baptized according to Catholic rites. The three condemned friends were allowed to smoke a cigarette together before their execution. Sophie was the first to be executed, followed by Christoph and Hans. As Hans was brought to the guillotine, he cried out, "Freedom will live!" The parents had left and returned to Ulm, hoping to somehow get the sentence commuted. But by 6 PM, their children had already been executed.

The Scholls' sister Inge went the next day to the apartment where her sister and brother had lived. She found Sophie's diary, which she took. Excerpts from the diary and Sophie's letters have been published.

The three first martyrs of the White Rose were buried in Perlach Cemetery in south Munich on February 24. After the execution, someone painted graffiti in Munich: "Their spirit lives." Later, the final leaflet was again distributed, this time with an extra line: "Despite everything, their spirit lives on."

MORE ARRESTS AND TRIALS

At the time of the Scholls' arrests, Franz Mueller was serving on the Western Front. Through a friend, he found out about the executions of Hans, Sophie, and Christoph. He immediately expected to be arrested, too, and tried to escape into France. But he was not successful. On one occasion, when he asked two French priests to help him, they asked him, "Why do you want to defect? You have to fight against the Communists. That is your duty." The priests seemed to like the fact that the Nazis were in their country, said Mueller.

The death of the Scholls had a major impact on Mueller. But "at this time death was a normal fate. In a few weeks I would be in Russia . . . The feeling of the nearness of death was like a narcotic state, a fatalistic state." For Mueller, death by execution was "a part of being against Hitler. He brought us to a point where we could not fulfill our lives, we could not stay alive."

When Mueller was finally arrested, his interrogation was simple—fourteen pages of "no, no, no." The trial itself lasted eleven hours. "Judge Freisler asked if I survived the trial, what profession would I choose. I said I wanted to be a Catholic priest. But I really wanted to study medicine. It was a primitive reaction because it meant I was not on his side. He was surprised. He paused and then said, 'Everyone can get into any profession in this state, but not with what you have done.'"

In the weeks following the execution of the Scholls and Christoph, there were a series of arrests. Alex tried to escape to Switzerland but returned because of deep snow. He was betrayed by a former girlfriend while in a shelter during an air raid in Munich. Also arrested were Traute LaFrenz, Eugen Grimminger, Falk Harnack, and several others who had helped the White Rose.

They were taken to Wittelsbach Palace.

On April 19, 1943, the same judge, Roland Freisler, tried Professor Huber, Alexander Schmorell, and Willi Graf. Another eleven friends were accused because they allegedly knew about the leaflets. The trial lasted fourteen hours. Huber, Schmorell, and Graf were sentenced to death that day. Ten others were sentenced to jail terms. Eugen Grimminger: ten years. Traute LaFrenz: one year. Harnack was released. George Wittenstein was interrogated by the Gestapo and later brought before a court martial. He was sent to the Italian front, where he was wounded, and returned to Germany at the end of the war.

The families of Schmorell, Huber, and Graf tried but failed to have their sentences commuted. Schmorell and Huber were executed on July 13, 1943. The Gestapo questioned Graf for a few more months and then put him to death on October 12, 1943.

In a third trial, book dealer Josef Sohngen was given a prison term for hiding leaflets in his cellar. Set free were architect Manfred Eickemeyer, accused of letting the group meet in his office; Harald Dohrn, Christoph Probst's father-in-law; and the painter Wilhelm Geyer, who was a friend of the Scholl family in Ulm. In a fourth trial, Willi Bollinger, who had disseminated the fifth leaflet, prepared false papers, and collected weapons, was sentenced to three months in jail.

In a fifth trial, on October 13, 1944, chemistry student Hans Leipelt, his girlfriend Marie-Luise Jahn and five other students were tried in Donauwoerth. Leipelt and Jahn had continued to disseminate the sixth leaflet, but they had not had contact with those who were executed. They also had collected money for the widow of Professor Huber, who had no income. Leipelt was given the death sentence and Marie-Luise Jahn got a twelve-year sentence. She was freed from prison by American soldiers. Three of the remaining five received prison terms, and two were released.

In the fall of 1943, the Gestapo uncovered student resistance groups in Hamburg. One had used the White Rose leaflets. Seven members of this group died in prison: Frederick Geuflenhainer, Elisabeth Lange, Kurt Ledien, Kathe Leipelt, Reinhold Meyer, Margarethe Mrosek, and Greta Rothe. Those who did not die of illness and hunger were killed at the end of the war without having been sentenced.

There were more trials in April 1943. In one of them, Heinz Kucharski was sentenced to death. He was saved by a bomb attack that took place as he was being taken to execution. Meanwhile, leaflets of the White Rose were still spreading throughout Germany and beyond. Copies were seen by Allied soldiers and even in concentration camps. Foreign newspapers applauded the actions of the German students. Did the students think that their goals would be achieved? "It is pretty hard to believe that good will triumph," says Traute LaFrenz. "But we certainly thought there would be an end to it in some form or other."

AN ENDURING LEGACY

How did people respond to the story after the war? Holocaust scholar Jud Newborn calls the case of the White Rose student resistance "a touchstone" for German ambivalence. "Even during the 1960s, while the members were being held forth as shining martyrs, the very same judges who had helped put them under the ax were still serving in the German judicial system," says Newborn, coauthor with Annette Dumbach of *Shattering the German Night: The Story of the White Rose*. "They just retired and got their pensions for the most part." In 2014, the guillotine used to execute Hans, Sophie, and Christoph was found in storage. It had been assumed destroyed or lost for many years. The fact that it had been so neglected reflects decades of ambiguity on coping with such a troubled history.

Now, however, the Scholls and the White Rose are revered throughout Germany for making the world aware of German resistance to the Nazi regime. "I think most Germans feel this subject [of German resistance] has been ignored by the rest of the world," says historian David Clay Large of

This bust of Sophie Scholl in the main building of Ludwig Maximilian University is one of many tributes to the sacrifices of the White Rose. Every year, the university also hosts a White Rose Memorial Lecture.

Montana State University.

To those who knew them, Hans and Sophie will always have a special place. Eyewitnesses

REMEMBERING
THEIR SACRIFICE

In 1997, a small White Rose memorial museum and archive was set up at the University of Munich where the friends studied. Books and pamphlets are available from that memorial. The exhibit has been translated into several languages and has traveled to other countries, from the United States to Russia. It is one of a few different places where people can pay tribute to those who lost their lives or livelihoods for participating in the White Rose, standing up what they knew to be right, and speaking up for those who couldn't speak for themselves.

Today, the main square of the university is called Geschwister-Scholl-Platz, named for Hans and Sophie, and a memorial immortalizing their leaflets can be seen there. In 2005, an Oscar-nominated German film entitled *Sophie Scholl – Die letzten Tage* (*Sophie Scholl – The Final Days*) was released. The Justizpalast, or Palace of Justice, where Hans, Sophie, and Christoph had their trial, opened a memorial in 2007 with documents and images related to the White Rose. Also in Munich is the Scars of Remembrance memorial wall with an inscription taken from a White Rose leaflet.

Paying tribute to the White Rose does not have to involve watching a movie or travel to these locations, however. Perhaps the most poignant way keep alive the legacy of Hans, Sophie, and their friends is to stand up to injustices and abuses, large and small, in our daily lives and continue their struggle. Human rights abuses, hate, violence, and oppression did not end with World War II, and tragically hold sway in many parts of the world today. However, the more we can educate ourselves on these issues and take action, the better chance there is for freedom and justice to prevail.

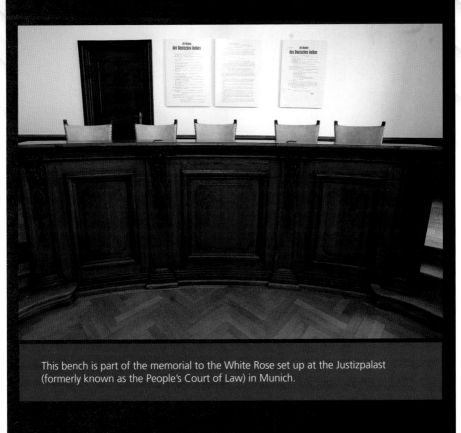

This bench is part of the memorial to the White Rose set up at the Justizpalast (formerly known as the People's Court of Law) in Munich.

Franz Mueller and Traute LaFrenz are not young anymore, although their memories of their friends remain fresh. Marie-Luise Jahn and George Wittenstein lived into their 90s before they passed. All have shared their recollections with younger generations, even though it was difficult and stirred up painful memories that some had kept quiet for years. More than 70 years after the end of World War II and the Holocaust, they remind us that both the horrors and the triumphs of the era cannot—and should not—be forgotten.

In their short life, the Scholls and the movement to which they were committed had a tremendous

This granite wall in Munich memorializes Germans, including the members of the White Rose, who had the courage to resist the Nazis and stand up for what was right.

impact on Germany and the world as a whole. The story of the Scholls and the White Rose is a lesson in dissent. It is a testimony to courage. And it is proof that anyone can make a difference. It is incumbent upon the rest of us to take up the torch they passed along and continue a tradition of speaking out against evil wherever it appears.

TIMELINE

October 24, 1893 Kurt Huber is born in Chur, Switzerland.

September 16, 1917 Alexander Schmorell is born in Orenburg, Russia.

January 2, 1918 Willi Graf is born in Kuchenheim, Germany.

September 22, 1918 Hans Scholl is born Ingersheim (now Crailsheim), Germany.

November 6, 1919 Christoph Probst is born in Murnau am Staffelsee, Germany.

May 9, 1921 Sophie Scholl is born in Forchtenberg, Germany.

January 1933 Adolf Hitler is appointed chancellor (prime minister) of Germany.

March 1933 Hitler assumes dictatorial powers. First concentration camp opens at Dachau.

August 1934 Hitler becomes commander in chief of the German armed forces.

November 1935 The Nuremberg laws are passed. Jews are stripped of their rights as German citizens.

July 1937 The Buchenwald concentration camp opens.

November 1938 During Kristallnacht, the "Night of Broken Glass," government-organized riots destroy Jewish homes, shops, and synagogues.

September 1939 German troops invade Poland, beginning World War II.

April 1940 The Auschwitz concentration camp opens.

September 1941 German Jews are ordered to wear yellow stars. Mass deportations to concentration camps begin.

January 1942 The Wannsee conference determines that the Final Solution for the Jewish people is to be mass extermination.

June 1942 The first leaflet of the White Rose movement is printed and distributed.

June–August 1942 Three more leaflets are distributed.

February 2, 1943 The Battle of Stalingrad ends.

February 18, 1943 Hans and Sophie are arrested after distributing copies of the sixth and final leaflet.

February 22, 1943 Hans Scholl, Sophie Scholl, and Christoph Probst are tried, found guilty of treason, and executed.

July 13, 1943 Alexander Schmorell and Kurt Huber are executed.

October 12, 1943 Willi Graf is executed.

June 1944 Allied forces invade Normandy.

February 1945 Auschwitz is abandoned by the Germans and captured by the Russians.

April 1945 American troops liberate Buchenwald and Dachau. Hitler commits suicide.

May 1945 Germany surrenders.

November 1945 The Nuremberg trials begin.

GLOSSARY

anti-Semitism Hatred or prejudice toward Jewish people.

Aryan A term used by Nazis to describe non-Jewish Caucasians with Nordic features whom they viewed as superior to all other races.

Communist Of or related to a political party that came to power in Russia in 1917 and was based on the principles of Marxist socialism and Marxist-Leninism, which aimed to dissolve private property and capitalism and replace them with state-owned means of production; also a member of this party.

concentration camp A place of internment kept in miserable conditions for those deemed political prisoners or undesirable to society, usually during times of war. In Nazi Germany and Nazi occupied territories, some camps were labor camps, where prisoners were forced to do hard manual labor, and others were extermination centers.

dictatorship An authoritarian form of government in which one person has total power over a country or state.

dissident Someone who disagrees with the way a government or other established organization is run.

Einsatzgruppen Special units of the German armed forces charged with finding and killing Jews and other undesirable groups in the territories occupied by the German army.

euthanasia "Mercy killing." In Nazi Germany, the term came to denote the practice of killing those individuals who are judged incapable of living worthwhile lives.

Führer Literally, the "Leader," the supreme head of the German government, who held absolute power. The position held by Adolf Hitler from 1933 to 1945.

genocide The systematic mass killing of all members of a particular racial, political, or cultural group.

Gestapo The German secret police, charged with locating and arresting Jews, political dissidents, and other opponents of the Nazi Party.

guillotine A machine with a sliding blade used to behead individuals sentenced to execution.

Holocaust The genocide of six million Jewish people and millions of others, including Gypsies and homosexuals, by the Nazis.

Lebensraum "Living space." The Nazi slogan associated with the belief that the inferior peoples of eastern Europe should be cleared away to make room for German expansion.

National Socialist The political party of Adolf Hitler, known less formally as the Nazi Party, which advocated the rearmament of Germany after World War I and the racial superiority of the German people.

passive resistance A method of opposing a government, law, or other authoritative measure, which emphasizes non-violent means of demonstration, including the refusal to obey certain laws.

propaganda False or exaggerated statements and ideas that are disseminated publicly to further the agenda of a political leader, cause, or government.

Reichstag The German parliament, or legislature, dissolved by Hitler in 1933.

SA (*Sturmabteilungen*) Storm Troopers, or SA or Brownshirts. Uniformed thugs under the control of the Nazi Party, used to incite street demonstrations and attack the Party's opponents. Hitler destroyed the SA after taking power.

Third Reich The term Nazis used to refer to the regime governing Germany from January 1933 to May 1945. The First Reich lasted from 800 to 1806 and the Second Reich from 1871 to 1918.

totalitarian Of or relating to a political philosophy that places the interests of the individual below those of the nation and exalts a society in which individuals are not allowed to disagree with authority, which generally belongs solely to a dictatorial government.

treason A crime that involves either trying to overthrow the government of one's own country, attempting to kill a head of state, or aiding a country's enemies at a time of war.

Center for White Rose Studies
Website: http://www.white-rose-studies.org
The Center for White Rose Studies preserves the
legacy of the White Rose members by using their
works to discuss informed dissent in today's
society. The organization performs and distrib-
utes research, offers speakers to various organizations, including schools, and provides other
resources to the public and scholars.

The Elie Wiesel Foundation for Humanity
555 Madison Avenue
New York, NY 10022
(212) 490-7788
Website: http://www.eliewieselfoundation.org
Founded by Elie Wiesel and his wife Marion soon
after he won the Nobel Peace Prize in 1986, this
foundation fights injustice and intolerance by
facilitating dialogue. The foundation also sup-
ports youth programs that highlight acceptance,
understanding, and equality.

The International Raoul Wallenberg Foundation
34 East 67th Street
New York, NY 10065
(212) 737-3275
Website: http://www.raoulwallenberg.net

The International Raoul Wallenberg Foundation
honors the legacy of Raoul Wallenberg and other
Saviors of the Holocaust by championing such
values as civic courage and solidarity, developing
education and outreach initiatives, and offering
various other resources.

Justizpalast (Palace of Justice)
Prielmayer Strasse 7
80335 Munich
Germany
+ 49 (0) 89 559703
Website: http://www.justiz.bayern.de/englisch.php
Members of the White Rose were tried in the
Volksgerichtshof, a building now known as the
Justizpalast in Munich. Room 253, where four of
the members were tried, is now a memorial for
the White Rose and is open to the public.

Montreal Holocaust Memorial Centre
5151, Chemin de la Côte-Sainte-Catherine
Montréal, QC H3W 1M6
Canada
(514) 345-2605
Website: http://www.mhmc.ca/en
Through its permanent collection of videos, testimonies, artifacts, and information about the
Holocaust, this museum and memorial seeks to
guide people of all age in learning about difficult
subjects including anti-Semitism, genocide, and
the Holocaust.

United States Holocaust Memorial Museum
100 Raoul Wallenberg Place SW
Washington, DC 20024-2126
(202) 488-0400
Website: http://www.ushmm.org
This museum stands as a source of information
about the events of the Holocaust as well as a
memorial to those who lost their lives during the
tragic event. In addition to their permanent and
temporary exhibits, the museum also maintains
an archive of video, interviews, and timelines
from the period.

USC Shoah Foundation
The Institute for Visual History and Education
650 West 35th Street, Suite 114
Los Angeles, CA 90089
(213) 740-6001
Website: http://sfi.usc.edu
The USC Shoah Foundation records interviews with
survivors and witnesses of the Holocaust and
other genocides and uses these recordings as
a means to educate and inspire action against
injustice. Since 1994, the Foundation has gathered 51,696 audio-visual testimonies in 32 different languages, all of which are available through
its online archives.

Vancouver Holocaust Education Centre
50-950 W 41st Avenue

Vancouver, BC V5Z 2N7
Canada
(604) 264-0499
Website: http://www.vhec.org
Founded in 1983 by Holocaust survivors, this
 Canadian teaching museum and leader in
 Holocaust education reaches more than 15,000
 students each year with its exhibits, programs,
 and teaching materials. The museum also has
 comprehensive resources, including a library,
 and maintains an archive of information about
 the Holocaust on its website.

White Rose Foundation
Ludwig Maximillians University of Munich
Geschwister-Scholl-Platz 1
80539 Munich
Germany
+49 (0) 89 2180 – 5678
Website: http://www.weisse-rose-stiftung.de/fkt_
 standard.php?aktion=cs&ma=cs&c_id=mamu-
 ra&topic=085&mod=17&page=1&lang=de
The White Rose Foundation educates young people today on the continued importance of
 the fight for human rights, for which many
 members of the White Rose lost their lives.
 The foundation has a permanent exhibition at
 the university at which many members of the
 White Rose were educated and traveling exhibits about the White Rose around the world.

The World Jewish Congress (WJC)
(212) 755-5770
Website: http://www.worldjewishcongress.org
The WJC was founded to mobilize Jews around
the world against the Nazi threat. It has since
come to represent and advocate for Jewish
communities in 100 countries around the
world for common interests.

WEBSITES

Because of the changing nature of Internet links,
Rosen Publishing has developed an online list of
websites related to the subject of this book. This site
is updated regularly. Please use this link to access
this list:

http://www.rosenlinks.com/HOLO/Scholl

FOR FURTHER READING

Bartrop, Paul. *Resisting the Holocaust: Upstanders, Partisans, and Survivors*. Santa Barbara, CA: ABC-CLIO, 2016.

Brezina, Corona. *Nazi Architects of the Holocaust*. New York, NY: Rosen Publishing, 2015.

Byers, Ann. *Kristallnacht and Living in Nazi Germany*. New York, NY: Rosen Publishing, 2015.

Cohen, Robert. *Jewish Resistance Against the Holocaust*. New York, NY: Rosen Publishing, 2015.

Darman, Peter. *The Holocaust and Life Under Nazi Occupation*. New York, NY: Rosen Publishing, 2013.

Darman, Peter. *World War II Begins*. New York, NY: Rosen Publishing, 2013.

Dearn, Alan. *The Hitler Youth: 1933–45*. Oxford, UK: Osprey, 2006.

Dumbach, Annette, and Jud Newborn. *Shattering the German Night: The Story of the White Rose*. Boston, MA: Little, Brown & Co, 1986.

Dumbach, Annette, and Jud Newborn. *Sophie Scholl and the White Rose*. Oxford, UK: Oneworld Publications, 2007.

Greek, Joe. *Righteous Gentiles: Non-Jews Who Fought Against Genocide*. New York, NY: Rosen Publishing, 2015.

Haffner, Sebastian. *Defying Hitler: A Memoir*. New York, NY: Farar, Straus and Giroux, 2003.

Hanser, Richard. *A Noble Treason: The Story of Sophie Scholl and the White Rose Revolt Against Hitler*. San Francisco, CA: Ignatius Press, 2012.

Hay, Jeff. *Genocide & Persecution: The Holocaust*. Detroit, MI: Greenhaven Press, 2014.

Jens, Inge, ed., and J. Maxwell Brownjohn, trans. *At the Heart of the White Rose: Letters and Diaries of Hans and Sophie Scholl*. New York, NY: Harper & Row, 1987.

Johnson, Eric A., and Karl-Heinz Reuband. *What We Knew: Terror, Mass Murder, and Everyday Life in Nazi Germany*. Cambridge, MA: Basic Books, 2005.

LaBella, Laura. *The Nuremberg Trials*. New York, NY: Rosen Publishing, 2015.

Machajewski, Sarah. *Elie Wiesel: Speaking Out Against Genocide*. New York, NY: Rosen Publishing, 2015. McDonough, Frank. *Sophie Scholl: The Real Story of the Woman who Defied Hitler*. Stroud, Gloucestershire, UK: History Press, 2010.

Meyer, Susan. *Nazi Concentration Camps: A Policy of Genocide*. New York, NY: Rosen Publishing, 2015.

Norton, James. *The Holocaust: The Jews, Germany, and the National Socialists*. New York, NY: Rosen Publishing, 2009.

Perl, Lila. *Great Escapes: The Holocaust*. Tarrytown, NY: Marshall Cavendish Benchmark, 2012.

INDEX

ABOUT THE AUTHOR

Lara Sahgal is a writer and editor based in Brooklyn. She majored in history in college, where she researched World War II extensively.

Toby Axelrod was a 1997-98 Fulbright scholar and award- winning journalist for the *New York Jewish Week*. Born in Queens, New York, she studied at Vassar College and the Columbia University Graduate School of Journalism.

PHOTO CREDITS

Cover, p. 21 Authenticated News/Archive Photos/Getty Images; p. 5 Ryan Donnell/Aurora//Getty Images; pp. 6-7 (background) Ingo JezierskiPhotographer's Choice/Getty Images; pp. 6-7 (inset) anahtiris/Shutterstock.com; pp. 10, 23, 38, 54, 77 Rolf E. Staerk/ Shutterstock.com; pp. 11, 80-81 Keystone-France/Gamma-Keystone/Getty Images; p. 13 Universal Images Group/Getty Images; p. 15 Popperfoto/Getty Images; pp. 18, 31, 36, 43, 45, 48, 64-65, 71, 83 ullstein bild/Getty Imagesp. 24 Mary Evans Picture Library/Everett Collection; pp. 26-27 Universal History Archive/UIG/Getty Images; p. 34 © Keystone Pictures USA/Alamy; p. 39 George Wittenstein/akg-images; pp. 41, 55, 72-73, 74 © INTERFOTO/Alamy; pp. 46-47 Mondadori/Getty Images; p. 61 Leoni Archive/Alinari Archives/Bridgeman Images; pp. 68-69 Hugo Jaeger/The LIFE Picture Collection/Getty Images; pp. 84-85, 93 Johannes Simon/Getty Images; p. 91 Raimund Kutter/imageb/imageBROKER/SuperStock; pp. 94-95 Gudjon E. Olafsson/Shutterstock.com; interior pages background textures and graphics Aleksandr Bryliaev/Shutterstock.com, kak2s/Shutterstock.com, argus/Shutterstock.com, Sfio Cracho/Shutterstock.com; back cover Ventura/Shutterstock.com.

Designer: Michael Moy; Editor: Shalini Saxena; Photo Researcher: Bruce Donolla